The Best Book of
Bugs

Claire Llewellyn

KINGFISHER

NEW YORK

Contents

KINGFISHER
LONDON & NEW YORK

Copyright © 2005 by Kingfisher
Published in the United States by Kingfisher,
175 Fifth Ave., New York, NY 10010
Kingfisher is an imprint of Macmillan Children's Books, London.
All rights reserved.

Distributed in the U.S. and Canada by Macmillan,
175 Fifth Ave., New York, NY 10010

Library of Congress Cataloging-in-Publication Data
Llewellyn, Claire.
Bugs / Claire Llewellyn.—1st ed.
p.   cm.
Includes index
Summary: Describes the habits and life cycles of various insects
and provides clues for identifying them in their natural habitats.
1. Arthropoda—Juvenile literature. 2. Insects—Juvenile
literature. [1. Insects.] I. Title.
QL437.2.L595   1998
595—dc21   97-39700   CIP AC

ISBN: 978-07534-5901-0

Kingfisher books are available for special promotions and
premiums. For details contact: Special Markets Department,
Macmillan, 175 Fifth Ave., New York, NY 10010.

For more information, please visit www.kingfisherbooks.com

Printed in China
10
10TR/0913/WKT/MAR(MAR)/128MA

A small world

Can you imagine what it's like to be very, very tiny? Millions of creatures are no bigger than your fingernail. For them, the grass is as thick as a forest and a flower is as tall as a tree.

Being small might sound scary, but it can be useful. Tiny bugs can hide anywhere—under a leaf, inside a nut, or deep in an animal's fur. There, they are safe from birds, frogs, and other sharp-eyed animals that feed on them.

Hiding places

Bugs live all around us, yet most of the time we don't even know that they are there. Look for them in the places where they like to hide—under a stone, inside a flowerpot, or in the crack of a wall.

A big collection

Flies

There are millions of different bugs and spiders, and they live all over the world. In fact, there are so many different types that scientists have sorted them into groups. Each group contains animals with the same type of body plan.

This book looks at bugs (or insects) and spiders. All bugs and spiders have a hard casing on the outside of their bodies called an exoskeleton. This protects an animal's soft insides, just like a strong suit of armor.

Wings and abdomen are hidden under hard wing cases.

Antenna

Head

Six legs

Thorax

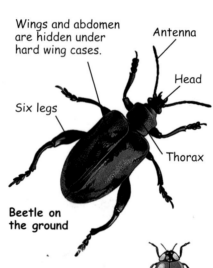

Beetle on the ground

Beetle in flight

Wing case

Bee

Abdomen

Wing

A ladybug is a type of beetle

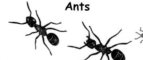

Ants

Bugs

All the creatures on this page—the beetles, bee, butterfly, true bugs, flies, and ants—are bugs. Ther are more bugs in the world than any other type of animal.

Butterfly

True Bugs

True bugs are a special type of bug with long, beaky mouthparts.

Many bugs look very different from one anothe but they all have three pairs of legs and three pa to their bodies—the head, thorax, and abdomen. Mc bugs also have wings, and most have long feelers called antennae.

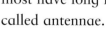

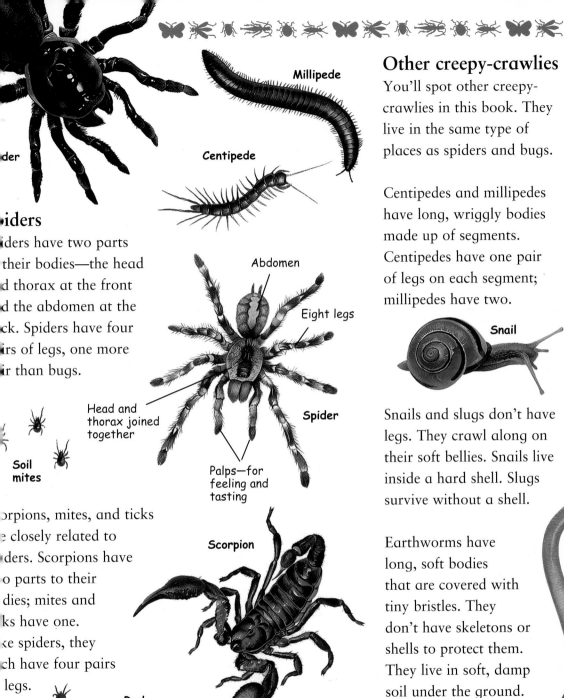

Millipede

Centipede

Other creepy-crawlies

You'll spot other creepy-crawlies in this book. They live in the same type of places as spiders and bugs.

Centipedes and millipedes have long, wriggly bodies made up of segments. Centipedes have one pair of legs on each segment; millipedes have two.

Snail

...iders

...iders have two parts ... their bodies—the head ...d thorax at the front ...d the abdomen at the ...ck. Spiders have four ...irs of legs, one more ...ir than bugs.

Abdomen

Eight legs

Head and thorax joined together

Spider

Palps—for feeling and tasting

Soil mites

...orpions, mites, and ticks ...e closely related to ...iders. Scorpions have ...o parts to their ...dies; mites and ...ks have one. ...e spiders, they ...ch have four pairs ... legs.

Scorpion

Red velvet mites

Snails and slugs don't have legs. They crawl along on their soft bellies. Snails live inside a hard shell. Slugs survive without a shell.

Earthworms have long, soft bodies that are covered with tiny bristles. They don't have skeletons or shells to protect them. They live in soft, damp soil under the ground.

Earthworm

7

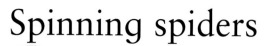

Spinning spiders

Web spider

Silk comes out through tiny tubes called spinnerets.

Strong, biting jaws

Palps to hold and taste prey

De[l] hai[r] leg[s]

Spiders are amazing creatures. They can make a silk that is stronger than steel and weave it into beautiful, lacy webs. The webs are important because many spiders have poor eyesight and their sticky traps help them catch their food. When an insect flies into the web, the spider feels it instantly through the hairs on its legs and rushes over for the kill.

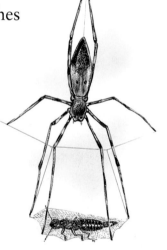

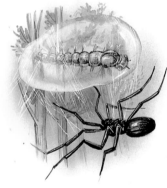

Sheet-web spider

A sheet-web spider spins a flat web with crisscrossing threads above it. Small bugs crash into the threads and fall on the web below.

Net-casting spider

A net-casting spider hangs head down and holds its silk web in its front legs. It throws the web over its prey like a net to trap it.

Water spider

A water spider lives in a be[ll] shaped web under the surfa[ce] of the water. It dashes out and seizes tiny creatures as they paddle by.

...en a struggling
...g is caught in its
...b, the spider injects
...with poison and wraps
...up tightly in silk. The
...ison kills the bug and
...ns it into a runny food
...t the spider sucks up like
...rink.

Spinning a web

Many spiders build a new web every day.

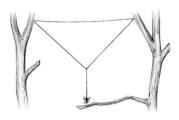

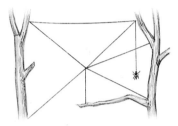

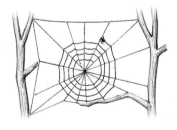

Garden spiders spin round orb webs. It usually takes them around an hour to make one.

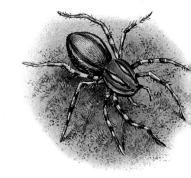

Hunting spiders

Hunting spiders chase, ambush, or leap on their prey. They don't use webs. They have sharp eyes to help them spot their prey and strong legs to help them catch it. Their jaws are good for biting. Some spiders also use their jaws to dig burrows, where they hide and lie in wait.

Wandering spider
The wandering spider doe have a home. It is always the move, hunting for a ta cockroach or caterpillar.

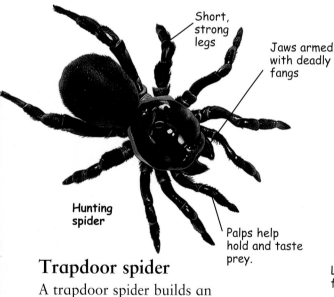

Short, strong legs

Jaws armed with deadly fangs

Hunting spider

Palps help hold and taste prey.

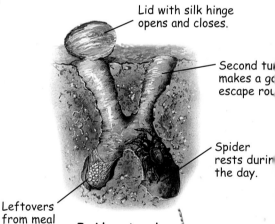

Lid with silk hinge opens and closes.

Second tu makes a g escape rou

Spider rests durin the day.

Leftovers from meal

Inside a trapdoor spider's burrow

Trapdoor spider
A trapdoor spider builds an underground burrow by shoveling away the soil with its jaws. Then it lines the burrow with silk, covers it with a lid, and camouflages it with twigs and grass. The lid keeps out enemies and the rain.

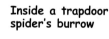

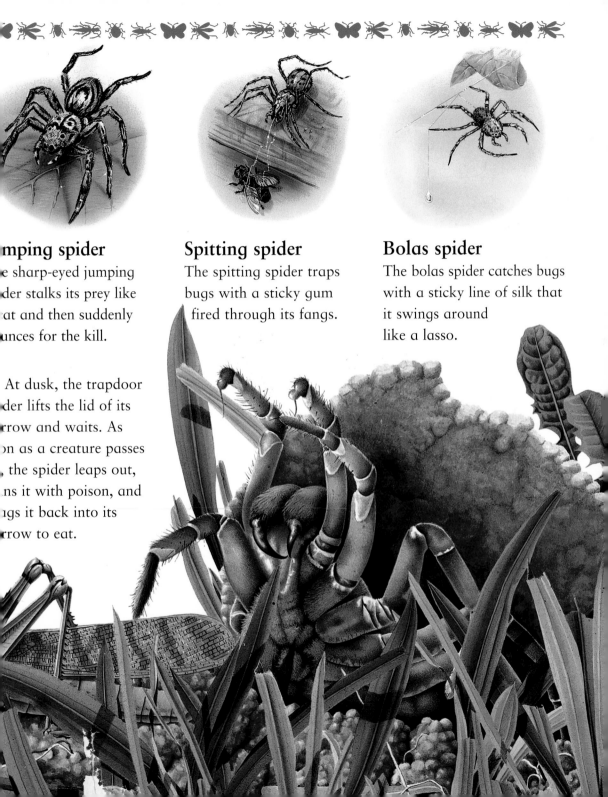

mping spider

e sharp-eyed jumping
der stalks its prey like
at and then suddenly
unces for the kill.

At dusk, the trapdoor
der lifts the lid of its
rrow and waits. As
on as a creature passes
, the spider leaps out,
ns it with poison, and
gs it back into its
rrow to eat.

Spitting spider

The spitting spider traps
bugs with a sticky gum
fired through its fangs.

Bolas spider

The bolas spider catches bugs
with a sticky line of silk that
it swings around
like a lasso.

Buzzing bees

Honeybees are busy all summer long. They fly from flower to flower, feeding on the sweet nectar inside. There are many different types of bees. Most of them live on their own, either in a burrow or a hollow stem. But honeybees live with thousands of others in a huge group called a colony. A colony works as a team. Together, the bees build a nest, find food, fight their enemies, and take care of their young.

A bees' nest

Honeybees build their nest in a cave or a hollow tree. Bees make a waxy material that they shape into long slabs called honeycomb. Bees' nests are strong and may last 50 years or more.

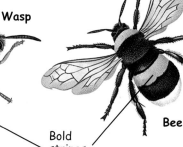

Wasp

Bee

Bold stripes warn of stinger.

A wasps' nest

Wasps' nest

Entrance

Wasps live in colonies, too. Every year, they build a new nest out of thin sheets of paper. They make the paper themselves by chewing tiny pieces of wood and mixing it with their saliva. The nest has a small doorway that is always guarded. The wasps keep their eggs and young safe inside.

A honeybee's year

Egg

Young larva

Full-grown larva

Pupa

Worker

Drone

Queen

1 In a honeybees' nest, most of the bees are females, called workers. A few of the bees are males, called drones. One of the bees is a queen.

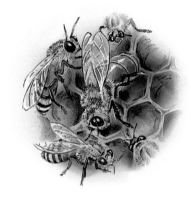

2 When she is young, th queen bee mates with the drones. Soon afterward, sh begins to lay thousands of eggs. She lays each egg in its own little pocket, or cell in the honeycomb.

3 After three days, the eggs hatch into wriggly grubs called larvae. The worker bees feed the larvae with nectar and pollen from flowers.

4 In a few days, the larv are full grown, and the workers seal their cells wit wax. Inside, each larva changes into a pupa, whic then becomes a bee.

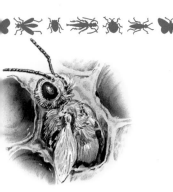  

The new bees start work
soon as they hatch.
ey clean the nest, feed
queen, and take care
the next batch of eggs.

6 As they grow older, the
young bees start to make
wax and build new slabs
of honeycomb to hold extra
food supplies for the winter.

7 During the summer,
the workers leave the nest
to gather food. They suck
sugary nectar from flowers
with their long tongues.

Pollen is a yellow dust
de by flowers. As they
, the bees comb pollen
o their back legs and
ry it back to the nest.

9 Inside the nest, the
nectar is turned into honey
and is stored in the cells.
The pollen is stored there,
too, in layers.

10 When a bee finds a new
source of food, it returns to
the nest and does a special
dance to tell the other bees
where they can find it, too.

If a bees' nest gets too
wded, the old queen flies
with a swarm of workers
start a new nest. A larva
the old nest grows into
ew queen.

12 Honeybees rest in the
winter, feeding on their
honey supply and staying
warm. In the spring, they
fly off in search
of more nectar.

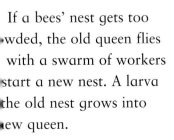

Hard-working ants

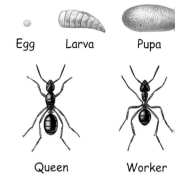

Egg Larva Pupa

Queen Worker

Ants make their nests under large stones or plants. Each nest contains hundreds of ants. One of them, the queen, lays all the eggs. The others are workers. They do different jobs around the nest such as feeding the larvae or gathering food. Ants eat all types of plants and animals. When they find food, they mark a trail back to the nest with a powerful scent, which the other ants quickly follow.

The queen ant

A queen ant has wings at first but pulls them out after she flies off to mate with a male. She spends the rest of her life laying hundreds of eggs.

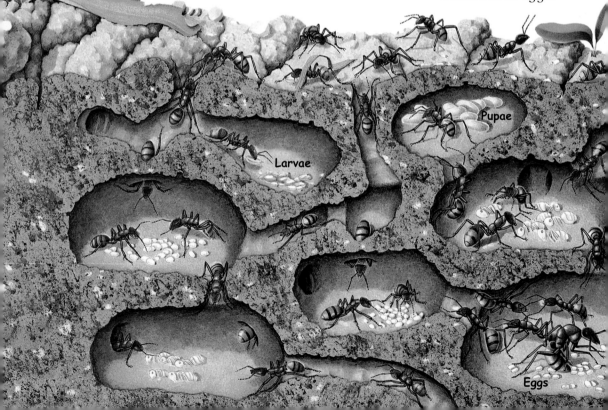

Larvae

Pupae

Eggs

An ants' nest

There are many different rooms inside an ants' nest. Some are nurseries for the eggs, larvae, and pupae. Others are used to store food or garbage.

Worker ants are always busy. Some take care of the queen and nurseries. Others guard the entrance to the nest, attack intruders, and search for food. Ants tap one another with their antennae to pass information.

eaver ants

aver ants work as a m to build their nest. ne of the ants hold leaves ether. Others bind the jes of the leaves together h sticky, silky thread de by their larvae.

Honeypot ants

Honeypot ants use some of their workers as jars. When flowers are plentiful, they fill the workers with nectar. They "milk" them when food is harder to find.

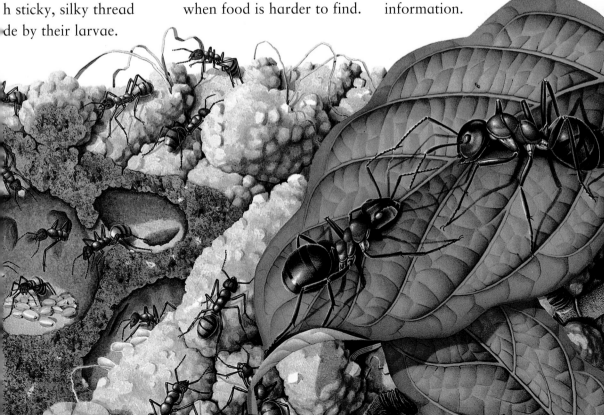

Busy beetles

All types of beetles crawl over the woodland floor, busily looking for food. Some munch on plants. Others are hunters that kill and eat other creatures or nibble on their rotting remains.

Beetles are small but very important. As they crawl and eat their way through the leaves, they mix dead plants and animals into the soil. This nourishes the soil and helps new plants grow.

Many other bugs live in woodlands, too, because there is plenty of food.

Jaws

Stag beetle

A beetle's bite

Many beetles have powerful jaws for grabbing, biting, and chewing their prey. This stag beetle is a male. Its huge jaws look like horns or antlers. It uses them to fight other males.

All types of beetles

Beetles are the largest group of animals in the world. There are more than 300,000 different types.

Most beetles have a hard, tough exoskeleton that protects them from their enemies. Some beetles are also armed with strong jaws or sharp spines.

Ladybugs

Many beetles are brightly colored to warn hungry enemies that they taste bad. A few are actually poisonous. Some beetles have stripes like a wasp. This helps keep enemies away, even though these beetles cannot sting.

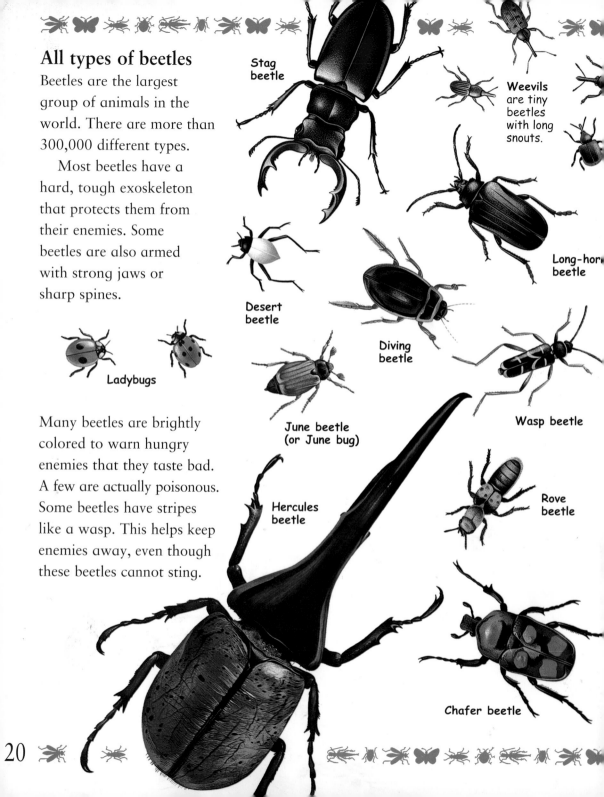

Stag beetle

Weevils are tiny beetles with long snouts.

Long-horn beetle

Desert beetle

Diving beetle

June beetle (or June bug)

Wasp beetle

Hercules beetle

Rove beetle

Chafer beetle

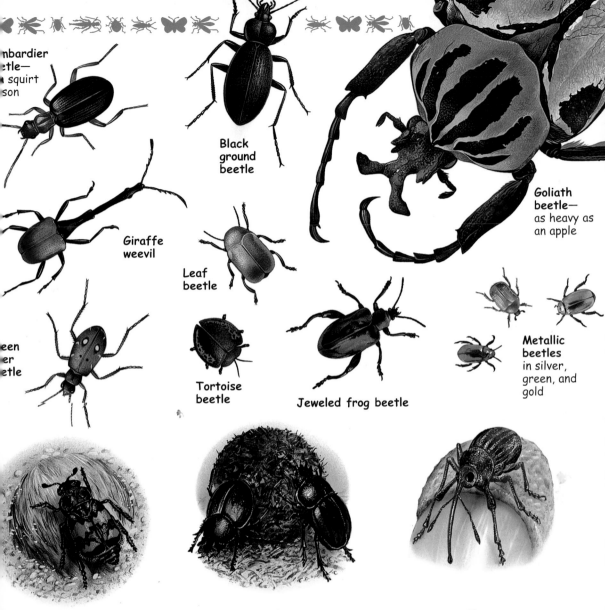

Bombardier
beetle—
a squirt
son

Black
ground
beetle

Goliath
beetle—
as heavy as
an apple

Giraffe
weevil

Leaf
beetle

Green
er
etle

Tortoise
beetle

Jeweled frog beetle

Metallic
beetles
in silver,
green, and
gold

Burying beetles

Burying beetles bury dead
animals and lay their eggs
on top. Their tiny larvae
then have plenty to eat.

Dung beetles

Dung beetles lay their eggs
inside balls of animal dung,
which they then bury under
the ground.

Nut weevils

Nut weevils drill holes in
nuts and lay their eggs
inside. The larvae eat the
nuts from the inside out.

Butterflies and moths

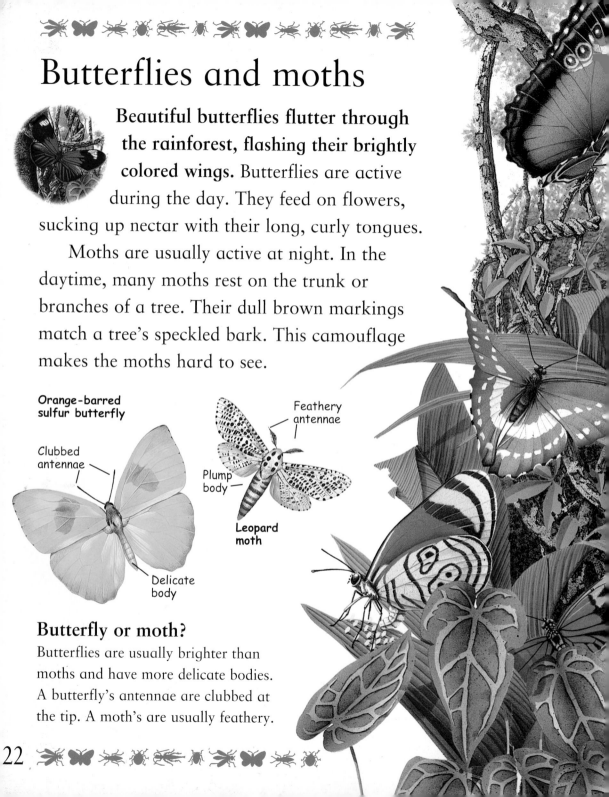

Beautiful butterflies flutter through the rainforest, flashing their brightly colored wings. Butterflies are active during the day. They feed on flowers, sucking up nectar with their long, curly tongues.

Moths are usually active at night. In the daytime, many moths rest on the trunk or branches of a tree. Their dull brown markings match a tree's speckled bark. This camouflage makes the moths hard to see.

Orange-barred sulfur butterfly

Clubbed antennae

Delicate body

Feathery antennae

Plump body

Leopard moth

Butterfly or moth?

Butterflies are usually brighter than moths and have more delicate bodies. A butterfly's antennae are clubbed at the tip. A moth's are usually feathery.

Egg to butterfly

Red admiral butterfly lays egg on leaf.

Caterpillar hatches from egg.

Caterpillar changes into pupa.

Butterfly dries wings in the air.

There are around 150,000 types of butterflies and moths, and they and their caterpillars come in all sorts of colors and sizes.

The Atlas moth is as big as a dinner plate. The Western pygmy blue butterfly is not much wider than your thumb.

Butterflies, like many bugs, change completely as they grow. This change is called metamorphosis.

Madagascan sunset moth

Apollo butterfly

Luna moth

Western pygmy blue butterfly

Cabbage white butterfly and caterpillar

Cairn's birdwing butterfly and caterpillar

Gypsy moth

88 butterfly

admiral
terfly

Orange-tip
butterfly

Atlas moth—
the largest
moth in the
world

Smooth
emerald
moth

allowtail
terfly and
erpillar

Comma
butterfly and
caterpillar

Common blue
butterfly and
caterpillar

Bright wings

The wings of butterflies and moths are covered with tiny scales that shimmer in the light. Some of them are brightly colored. Others have bold patterns or scary eyespots. When a butterfly or moth flashes its wings at its enemies, it confuses them and gives itself time to escape.

Owl moth

Hornet moth

Darting dragonflies

Life in a pond is not as peaceful as it seems. Huge dragonflies dart noisily through the air, snatching at flies. Dainty damselflies flash like jewels in the sun as they snap at gnats and midges. Other hunters live in the water itself and pounce on anything that moves.

Egg to dragonfly

A dragonfly begins its life as an egg in the water. The egg hatches into a fierce creature called a nymph, which lives and grows in the pond. After a year or two, the nymph climbs out of the water onto a plant.

There its skin splits open, and a new dragonfly crawls out. Not every small creature leaves the pond. Some, like water scorpions and spiders, spend their entire lives under the water.

Catching a meal

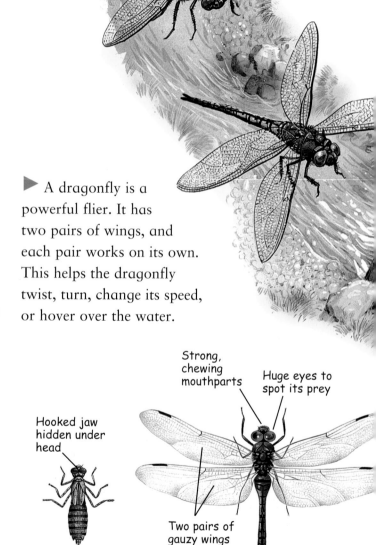

1 A dragonfly nymph lurks deep in the pond, hidden by its muddy colors. Suddenly a tadpole swims past.

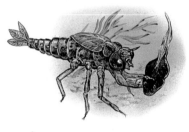

2 Quickly, the nymph shoots out a pair of sharp, hooked jaws and grabs its prey.

▶ A dragonfly is a powerful flier. It has two pairs of wings, and each pair works on its own. This helps the dragonfly twist, turn, change its speed, or hover over the water.

Strong, chewing mouthparts

Huge eyes to spot its prey

Hooked jaw hidden under head

3 The nymph's deadly jaws slide back to its mouth, and the hunter feeds on its catch.

Two pairs of gauzy wings

Dragonfly nymph

Adult dragonfly

Damselfly nymph

Adult damselfly

Living on water

All animals need oxygen. Some pond creatures get oxygen from the water. Others get it from the air.

Like dragonflies, damselflies and caddis flies lay their eggs in ponds. A damselfly egg hatches into a nymph. A caddis fly egg hatches into a larva.

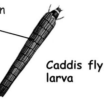
Larva hides in a silk tube, which it camouflages with plants and stones.
Caddis fly larva

A damselfly nymph has three gills on its tail, which soak up oxygen in water.

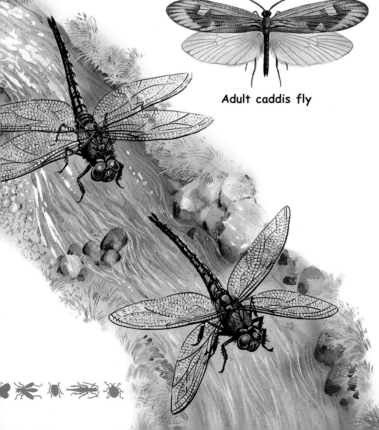
Adult caddis fly

A water scorpion floats to the surface of the water and takes in air through a tube.

A diving beetle collects air bubbles and stores them under its wings.

Out at night

Summer nights are alive with all types of bugs. Crickets chirp, mosquitoes hum, and tiny fireflies flash in the dark. This is their way of sending signals to one another.

Night is a good time for bugs because the air is cool and many of their enemies are asleep. Through the hours of darkness, these tiny creatures feed, hunt, and look for a mate. At dawn they hide, and the bees, butterflies, and other sun-loving creatures return with the warmth and light.

Glossary

abdomen The back part of a bug's body. Inside the abdomen is the heart and the various parts that break down food and help a creature produce its young.

antenna (*plural* antennae) One of a pair of feelers that pick up scents and tastes in the air and help an animal feel its way around.

bug (or insect) An animal with three parts to its body and three pairs of jointed legs.

camouflage The colors and markings on an animal that help it blend in with its surroundings and make it difficult to see.

colony A large group of animals that live together. Honeybees live in a colony, as do ants.

drone A male honeybee, whose only job is to mate with the queen.

exoskeleton The hard casing on the outside of the body of most bugs.

fang The clawlike part of a spider's jaws that it uses to stick into an animal and inject poison.

gill The part of an animal's body that allows it to breathe under the water. The gills soak up oxygen that has dissolved in the water. The nymphs of water bugs, such as damselflies, have gills.

grub Another name for the legless larva of an insect.

larva (*plural* larvae) The young stage of an insect after it hatches from an egg, which looks very different from an adult. A larva has to pass through a pupa stage before it becomes an adult bug.

metamorphosis The change from a young bug into an adult bug—for example, from a caterpillar to a butterfly.

nectar The sugary juice inside flowers that attracts bugs and other small animals. Bees use nectar to make honey.

nymph The young stage of a bug, such as a grasshopper or a dragonfly, that changes gradually into an adult without passing through a pupa stage.

oxygen A gas that all animals need to breathe in order to survive. Oxygen is one of the gas found in the air and water.

palp One of a pair of feelers nec the jaws of a spider or a bug tha feel and taste its food.

pollen The yellow dustlike pow made by flowers. When bu carry it to the same type of flowers, the can make seeds.

pupa (*plural* pupae) The stage in a bug's life when it changes from a larva to an adult. In butterflies and moths, the pupa is called the chrysalis.

thorax The middle part of a bug's body, in between the hea and the abdomen. A bug's wing and legs are attached to the thorax.

true bug A group of bugs with a long, sharp feeding tube, which they use to pierce animals or plants and suck out their juices.